Congruent

Bethany Simpson

Presentation by *BookLeaf Publishing*

Web: www.bookleafpub.com

E-mail: info@bookleafpub.com

ISBN: 9789357442589

First edition 2023

For Chad.

*For all the steps we've taken and the journey
still to come.*

ACKNOWLEDGEMENT

Many people have directly and indirectly helped me with the writing of this book. I would like to take this opportunity to thank them.

Chad, you have been patient and kind to me throughout this year. We have been told many times that the first year is the hardest, and while I can see the truth in that, there is no one I would rather have gone through this year with. Thank you for encouraging me to go for this writing challenge and to publish my poetry. You have been an inspiration to me, I love you.

To my sister, Angela, thank you for putting up with my drama! You have been a shoulder to cry on, a listening ear, a loving hug, and most importantly the best big sister I could ask for! Thank you for all your guidance and encouragement with my poetry throughout the years but especially with this book. I couldn't have done this without you.

I would like to thank my parents for raising me and loving me – all the versions of me! For supporting me throughout the ups and downs of life and for showing me how to build a strong marriage. Thank you, especially for your sacrifices, journeys, and phone calls over the past year to support us. You are a true blessing.

To my in-laws, thank you for welcoming me into the family. It has been a blessing to get to know you and see our families grow together this past year. I look forward to many more years of this in the future.

To my friends thank you for the great experiences that we've shared, and the support and love that you have shown me through this time of change. While I may be further away now, I look forward to this new chapter, where the distance does not separate us, but rather makes our meetings all the sweeter. I love and appreciate you all.

And finally, most importantly, I would like to thank God, without whom this would not have been possible. God bless you all.

PREFACE

In March 2022, I got married, moved house, and changed my job all at the same time. While all of these things were moments of great joy for me, they also came with challenges, and lessons and set me on a path that held a lot of discovery. The year that followed was one of emotional reconnection, reorganising, and healing. Looking back over that time has inspired these poems. I have traced through some of the key moments of that journey, retracing the challenges, successes, and emotions I went through, rediscovering the lessons that were tucked away within them all.

I hope that these poems may connect with you, wherever you are and whatever journey you are on.

God bless you.
Bethany.

Beginnings

I've prayed & I've cried
I've fallen & I've tried
And though first steps are the hardest
The journey is worth it all.

Starlight

Covered in starlight
Half dazed from the day,
Drunk on your smile
and these sweet memories.
A short walk, a vow,
A tear mixed with a grin,
A crescendo of joy
and a new life begins.

Kiss Me

Kiss me
Underneath the stars
As the music fades away.
Let us dance
'Neath the night sky
At the closing of the day.

You, Me and the Sea

In our own little bubble
Far away from trouble
Just you, me and the sea.
From the handsome Colosseum
to the old German museums
to just you, me and the sea.
A small boat in Venice,
gliding by the terrace,
it was just you, me and the sea.
Pizza by candle light in Rome
Then wandering this portside Greek town
Yes, just you, me and the sea.
And last before we ventured home
Athena smiled from her hillside realm
on you, me and the sea.

Your Arms

I had these walls built around me,
So high and thick to protect me from
The world and wind outside.
I kept myself locked inside,
Safe from the battering rams and
The chaos that is just beyond the door.

And then you came.

There you were, knocking on the door,
Taking down the walls brick by brick,
And your gentleness scared me.
No one had treated me so kindly,
Had touched my skin without scarring,
But healed the wounds instead.

And as those walls came down
And the world tumbled through
And crashed all around me, screaming.

There you were.

Your arms around me, protecting me

Like walls

Softly holding, pulling me near,
Holding me together, away from the fire.

Tired

I love the way you look when you are tired,
When you're fighting with all your strength to
stay awake.
When you're negotiating a closing time with
your eyelids
Because you know falling asleep now would be
a mistake.
I love the way you look when you are tired,
There's a stillness that seems to wash across
your face
Like the day has been done and all the tasks
accomplished
And now all that's left to do is find our peace.
I love the way you look when you are tired,
And the way your hushed voice whispers out
"Goodnight".
Though you fight the words and wish you didn't
need them,
I know you'll find your voice once more in the
morning light.

Goodbyes

I'm not good at "Goodbyes" - I never have been.
They stick in my throat and fog up my eyes until
I can't see. This was the worst of all - all at once,
all together, waited for so long and yet here too
soon.
Gathered, we talked of so many things, dreams
and memories, until the sun gave way to the
stars and that word was all that was left.
Hanging in the air, waiting to be claimed, or to
claim me.
I've boxed up those memories. I'll take them
with me. I'll hold them close like you're holding
me now.
"Don't be a stranger"
A stranger. Is that what these miles will make
me? Is distance all it takes to dim a memory, to
turn a friend into a stranger, a home into a
house?
Or can "Goodbye" herald the coming of a new
dawn, the charting of a new path, where home is
not a location but the people. While miles may
separate us they are only miles and nothing is
lost in these "Goodbyes".

Dress me in Yellow

Dress me in yellow and paint me a smile,
Just hold me close and stay for a while.
My hands are shaking and my legs are so weak,
My throat feels so hoarse from trying to speak.
The clouds they keep rolling and I'm trying to
see,
The blue sky I know that is waiting for me.
I know the sun shines even when shaded from
view,
So, I'll sit for a while and wait here with you.
Wait for my heart to stop breaking each beat,
Wait for the steady to return to my feet.
So, dress me in yellow and paint me a smile,
Yes, just hold me close and stay for a while.

Hold Me

Hold me -
Just that and nothing more.
I've come undone again today,
My pieces scattered across the floor.
Hold me -
Firm and sure within your arms.
The world is loud again today,
Will you keep me safe from harm?
Hold me -
Curl me close towards your heart.
Squeeze the broken pieces back together,
Please don't let me fall apart.

Congruent

I don't feel like myself today
But I've painted on this smile -
Over the cracks and the crumbling,
Over the broken and the breaking -
So that you won't see through me.
This smile is my armour,
Shielding me from the cloud
That threatens to swarm in and
Drown me in the tears that wait
Just behind my eyes.
I know that this will pass so I
Paint on this smile and tell you
I'm fine,
While the storm rages on.
I don't feel like myself today.

Boundaries

My life was an open book
For everyone to see.
But I've found that there is wisdom,
In reserving pages just for me.

Breathe

Take a breath,
Close your eyes,
Just listen to the waves,
The wind,
Feel the way it brushes your skin,
folding around you like an old friend.
Take a breath,
Close your eyes,
Just listen to the rain,
Fall down,
As it dances on the ground
And beats out it's ever gentle rhythm.
Just breathe,
Close your eyes,
Far away from the noise,
Be still,
Just breathe.

Mundane

14

We think of life, of love, in big, grand moments.
In New Year's parties, in Hollywood romances,
white sand beaches, fireworks and flames under
the night sky.
We think of it as sweeping, ever moving, like an
action movie - keep me entertained, leave them
wanting more.
Life, love, is so much more than that. It is
Tuesday afternoons, the car drive home,
housework, building life together, lazy coffees
on the sofa while the hours drift by. These are
not grand moments but I love you in these
moments. In every ordinary, mundane second.
That is life. That is love.

Burnt out

I'm tired.
I've been tired for a long time.
Tired of trying:
Trying to spin these plates,
Trying to live up to everyone else's expectations,
Trying to hold on to my dreams,
And who I feel I should be
I'm tired.
Tired of making mistakes,
Tired of being told it'll make me stronger,
Tired of being told to pick myself back up,
Dust myself off
And try again
Without any hope of respite
I'm tired.
Tired of not knowing the answers,
Tired of the weight of expectation,
Tired of the weight of the world,
Tired of hating myself relentlessly,
Tired of being tired.
I'm so tired...

Flowers

How do flowers grow if no one prunes them?
If there is no rain how will they survive?
And while pruning dead ends may be painful,
It's done to keep the flower alive.

Kintsugi

In Japan they repair broken things with gold.
It is a beautiful reminder that the journey is a
part of the process; every crack, every break,
every chip has its place.
We are so quick to hide our journey, to mask the
marks that make us who we are.
No journey is without its troubles - not a journey
that is worth travelling.
Yet we cover them, we hide them, presenting the
perfect, polished, glazed version of ourselves.
But what if we were to line our cracks with
gold?
To hold them to the light and call them
beautiful?
What if, instead of shutting ourselves away, we
embraced each stumble, stood back up stronger,
lining it with beauty and grace?
With gold.

The Edge

The edge,
Where the wind blows through my hair, across
my skin, fills my lungs.
Where eternity stretches out before me.
Where I've become accustomed to belonging.
The edge,
Where I cling to the roots I've grown, so I can
find my way back home. Surrounded by walls
and brick and security.
The edge,
Where I watch the sun set as it mellows my
heart and I breathe deep as a day dies and a new
life is born just over the edge.

This Face

I love the face I make when I am happy.
I don't mean "smile for the camera" happy,
I mean truly, fully, unapologetically,
laugh-till-your-sides-are-splitting,
the-skies-will-never-be-grey-again happy.
The way I grin so widely that I show my huge
teeth in a way that usually I would never do.
The way my smile stretches so far across my
face that my cheeks jump forward to escape
being crushed by the joy.
The way my eyes burst with colour while I
scrunch them up at the same time.
Yes, I love the way I look when I am truly
happy.
I didn't always love it.
I used to hate that face.
I used to hate smiling with my mouth open -
My teeth are too big, I thought, I look weird,
My eyes squint behind my glasses,
I just look odd, so I'll smile like they do on
magazines.
Let's take that picture just one more time,
We have to make sure I look right.
You can't put that online!
What if someone sees?!

Delete it!
So many messages I'd absorbed of how I needed
to look, act, think, feel,
Until I told myself the same thing day in and day
out.
Then that one fateful photograph.
The end of a stressful weekend,
But that had culminated in the most amazing
experience,
Caught off guard,
The camera broke through
Through the noise, the messages, the lies,
And it caught me,
Off guard,
On point,
In truth,
My truth,
My unapologetic truth,
The joy I felt radiating through into my face.

I didn't see that picture for a few months
But when I did, I realised, and I keep realising,
I love this, awkward, "unattractive", beautiful,
unapologetically, happy face.

I Learned to Waltz Last Night

I learned to Waltz last night
I glided through the air,
The world it simply disappeared
As music mixed with light.
I learned to Waltz last night
And we danced through lights like stars,
Like the world was our stage solely
And the music seemed only ours.
I learned to Waltz last night
My feet stumbled to the one, two, three,
But soon my fear it crumbled
And I found myself to be free.
I learned to Waltz last night
We danced till the sun arose.
Some sang and others played;
Keys twinkled and jazz flowed.
My worries fell away last night
As I danced through the lights,
And whilst I know tomorrow's coming
I learned to Waltz last night.

Rushing

I've always been in a rush to get where I'm
going.
To futures imagined and dreams realised.
To see wishes fall from their stars bursting to life
before my eyes.
I've lived in daydreams of how things will be; in
a daze of worlds not yet come true.
But I realise that one day I will look back,
wondering where the time went.
What happened to the good old days?
When did youth slip by me and through my
fingers, did I so easily let it pass me by?
So, I will learn to treasure, not the dreams of
tomorrow, but the moments of today.
Each second, each minute, I shall not miss.
I shall learn to look upon each moment without
wishing for the next,
Embracing the stillness of each breath you
breathe, each beat of your heart.
For one day I shall want to recall them all.
I will trawl through the pictures of my mind for
such a moment as this;
Dancing in the kitchen, a lazy afternoon in your
arms, a walk in the early morning mist.

The future will come soon enough, dreams will
become reality or be traded for other dreams, but
time ticks on regardless.
Now is a time I will never have again and so;
I shall keep each moment without rushing to the
next.

The Journey

For all the steps we've taken
And the journey still to come,
I know as long as you are with me
There I'll find my home.